SPORTS ALL-ST★RS

KEVIN DURANT

Jon M. Fishman

Lerner Publications ◆ Minneapolis

Lerner Publications Company
A division of Lerner Publishing Group, Inc.
241 First Avenue North
Minneapolis, MN 55401 USA

For reading levels and more information, look up this title at www.lernerbooks.com.

Main body text set in Albany Std 15/22. Typeface provided by Agfa.

Library of Congress Cataloging-in-Publication Data

Names: Fishman, Jon M., author.
Title: Kevin Durant / Jon M. Fishman.
Description: Minneapolis, MN : Lerner Publications, 2017. | Series: Sports All-Stars | Includes bibliographical references and index. | Audience: Age 7–11. | Audience: Grade 4 to 6.
Identifiers: LCCN 2016050976 (print) | LCCN 2016055912 (ebook) | ISBN 9781512434538 (lb : alk. paper) | ISBN 9781512456165 (pb : alk. paper) | ISBN 9781512450873 (eb pdf)
Subjects: LCSH: Durant, Kevin, 1988—Juvenile literature. | Basketball players— United States—Biography—Juvenile literature. | African American basketball players—Biography—Juvenile literature.
Classification: LCC GV884.D868 F57 2017 (print) | LCC GV884.D868 (ebook) | DDC 796.323092 [B]—dc23

LC record available at https://lccn.loc.gov/2016050976

Manufactured in the United States of America
1-42102-25396-3/7/2017

CONTENTS

The New Guy 4

Growing Star 8

Keep Climbing 12

Paying Off. 18

Like a Warrior. 24

All-Star Stats 28

Source Notes 29

Glossary 30

Further Information 31

Index 32

THE NEW GUY

Kevin Durant takes a shot against the San Antonio Spurs.

Fans were quiet as they shuffled out of Oracle Arena in Oakland, California. The San Antonio Spurs had just crushed Kevin Durant's Golden State Warriors, 129–100. This was not how Durant's first game with his new team was supposed to go. It was the first day of the 2016–2017 National Basketball Association (NBA) season. The Spurs were a good team. But most fans thought the Warriors would be better.

In the 2015–2016 regular season, the Warriors were by far the best team in the league. They won their 73rd game on the last day of the season. No NBA team had ever won as many games in a single season. But the Cleveland Cavaliers beat them in the NBA Finals.

Golden State fans were ready to cheer for their new superstar. Durant had played his entire NBA career with the Oklahoma City Thunder. Warriors fans remembered that Durant was voted NBA Most Valuable Player (MVP) in 2013–2014. They knew he had played in seven NBA All-Star Games. They were thrilled by his 28.2 points per game in 2015–2016—third best in the NBA that year. But they just wanted him to win a game with his new team.

The Warriors played again three days later. This was how the 2016–2017 season was supposed to go. Durant hit shots from all around the court against the New Orleans Pelicans. Teammate Stephen Curry did the same. But Pelicans star Anthony Davis scored 21 points in the first half. He kept the game close.

Durant kept sinking shots in the second half. Golden State had a small lead with less than a minute to play in the game. Davis stepped forward for a long shot. But Durant was there. He swatted the ball and took off with it down the court. He stepped between two defenders for a **layup**.

The play sealed the victory for Golden State, 122–114. Fans cheered the first of many wins for Durant and the Warriors in 2016–2017. It was going to be a great season.

Durant keeps the ball away from New Orleans Pelicans player Buddy Hield (left).

In 2005, Durant competed at a camp with some of the best high school players in the country.

Kevin Wayne Durant was born in Suitland, Maryland, on September 29, 1988. Suitland is near Washington, DC. He grew up with his mother, Wanda. Kevin has a sister named Brianna and brothers named Tony and Rayvonne. Kevin's father, Wayne, didn't live with the family. But he stayed in close contact with his son.

Kevin was a tall, skinny boy. Kids at school teased him about his height. His grandmother, Barbara, told him not to worry about it. She said his height was a blessing.

Kevin's mother, Wanda, was with him when he was drafted by the Seattle SuperSonics in 2007.

Kevin and Tony spent a lot of time at their grandmother's house. But Wanda wanted her kids to be more active when they weren't in school. She signed the boys up for basketball at nearby Seat Pleasant Activity Center. At first, Kevin wasn't sure he wanted to play basketball. That changed as soon as he arrived at the gym. "Once I opened that door, it was like I was at an amusement park or something," he said.

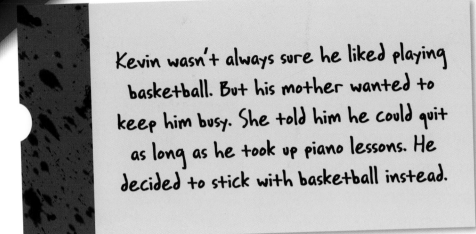

Kevin wasn't always sure he liked playing basketball. But his mother wanted to keep him busy. She told him he could quit as long as he took up piano lessons. He decided to stick with basketball instead.

It didn't take long for Kevin to become a big-time basketball **prospect**. His height helped. He stood 6 feet 2 inches (1.9 meters) tall as a high school freshman in 2002. Then he grew 7 inches (18 centimeters) by the time he was a senior. At 6 feet 9 inches (2.1 m), he towered over most of the players trying to defend him. His grandmother had been right: his height was a blessing.

As a senior, Kevin averaged more than 23 points and 10 **rebounds** each game. He was one of the top three high school basketball prospects in the country. Colleges with great teams such as Duke University wanted Kevin. He chose the University of Texas.

At Texas, Durant blossomed into a national star. In 2006–2007, he averaged almost 26 points and more than 11 rebounds per game. Texas won 25 games and a place in the **National Collegiate Athletic Association (NCAA) men's basketball tournament**. Less than two months later, Durant joined the NBA **Draft**. The Seattle SuperSonics chose him with the second overall pick. In 2008, the team moved to Oklahoma and became the Oklahoma City Thunder.

Durant charges down the court in a University of Texas game against the Texas Southern Tigers.

KEEP CLIMBING

Durant shoots hoops during training.

The Hill, as Kevin calls it, is a steep street near his grandmother's house.

As a high school athlete, Kevin's coach made him run up the Hill. Then he walked down—backward.

He did it over and over again. His mother often waited for him in the car, reading a book. Sometimes she told Kevin to keep running so she could finish a chapter.

"I know when I have a son and he wants to play basketball [the Hill] is the first place I'm going to send him," Durant said. "I'm looking forward to that day."

Kevin's mom has been a big support his entire life.

Durant hasn't stopped climbing since his days on the Hill. He worked hard as a young player to add weight to his body. He started a new meal plan as a **rookie** in the NBA. Durant could still eat the same food he loved—he was just supposed to eat more of it. "Four eggs instead of two," he said. "Four pieces of baked chicken instead of two. Four meals instead of three."

More food helped Durant get bigger. Working out helped him get stronger.

Durant never stops training and practicing his shooting.

He still works with **trainers** to target all of his muscles. Moves such as **lunges** make his legs powerful and allow him to soar to the basket. Exercises with **dumbbells** and other weights keep his arms and upper body in top shape.

Durant went to practice sessions while he played for the 2015 USA Men's National Team.

Durant and LeBron James (right) played together for Team USA during the 2012 Summer Olympics.

Durant still does a lot of running. He likes to run on sand. It takes more energy to run across soft sand. The uneven surface also helps Durant improve his balance. He often runs with former teammate Russell Westbrook. Durant says the two are "like brothers."

Another of Durant's workout partners is NBA icon LeBron James. In the NBA off-season, Durant and James get together for some serious work. They practice skills together on the court. And, of course, they run. The two superstars push each other to work even harder.

Durant is close friends with his former Oklahoma City Thunder teammate Russell Westbrook (right).

Durant has a contract to promote the Nike brand.

Durant has gotten rich in the NBA—really rich. His basketball salary has gone up every year he's been in the league. In 2007–2008, he made more than $4 million. By 2011–2012, he earned about $15 million for the season. In 2015–2016, he made more than $20 million.

But Durant's money from the NBA is just the beginning. When he joined the league, he also signed a deal to **endorse** Nike. The shoe company agreed to pay him about $60 million over seven years. When the deal ended, Nike signed Durant again. This time, they agreed to pay him $300 million over 10 years! He also has deals with Foot Locker and other companies.

Durant uses some of his money to help young people succeed. He knows that sports can be an important part of a happy childhood. "When I was young, playing basketball was one of the things that kept me out of trouble," he said.

Durant wore these Nike shoes while he played for the Oklahoma City Thunder.

On the Screen

If you turn on your TV, there's a decent chance that Kevin Durant will be on it. Fans have seen him in basketball games and on shows such as *SportsCenter* for years. On a high-profile team such as the Warriors, he'll be on TV more than ever.

Durant also appears in lots of commercials. He's been in countless TV ads for Nike. And maybe you've seen his fun ads for Panini trading cards or the *NBA 2K17* video game. An ad for American Family Insurance with National Football League (NFL) star J. J. Watt shows the two athletes surprising fans.

Durant also goes to events, such as this 2016 Nike event in China.

Durant shoots against Anthony Davis (left) and Lance Stephenson (right) during a 2016 game against the New Orleans Pelicans.

Durant meets with young fans during a charity event.

The Kevin Durant Charity Foundation tries to improve the lives of children through sports and education. One of the foundation's projects is making sure more young people have access to good basketball courts. Durant makes lots of visits to schools and other places to talk about his foundation.

Durant's success on the court has made him a big star off of it too. He has appeared on popular TV shows such as *Jimmy Kimmel Live!* and *Good Morning America*. In 2014, he won the ESPY award for Best NBA Player. He was also voted Best Male Athlete that year.

Durant accepts the award for Best Male Athlete at the 2014 ESPY Awards.

LIKE A
WARRIOR

Durant goes
for the dunk!

NBA fans expect a lot when you're the second overall pick in the draft as Durant was. They want you to be a star, and they want you to be a star *right now*. Durant didn't keep them waiting. In 2007–2008, he scored more than 20 points per game and was voted NBA Rookie of the Year. In the eight full seasons since then, he has never scored fewer than 25 points per game.

Durant dunks while playing for the Oklahoma City Thunder.

Rookie of the Year. All-Star Game MVP. NBA MVP. The list of Durant's awards and honors goes on and on. But the true measure of a superstar is how much better he makes his team. The 2007–2008 Seattle SuperSonics won just 20 games. They won 23 in Oklahoma City the next year. In 2009–2010, they broke through with 50 wins. But they lost in the first round of the playoffs.

In the 2010–2011 season, the Thunder went deep into the playoffs. They made it to the NBA Finals in 2011–2012 before losing to the Miami Heat for the championship. Durant had helped make the Thunder into one of the league's top teams.

Durant and Golden State Warrior teammate Stephen Curry (right) make a powerful team.

Durant became a **free agent** after the 2015–2016 season. He says he signed with Golden State because it was the best place for him to grow as a player. He also had gotten comfortable in Oklahoma and wanted to challenge himself with something new. Joining a superstar like Stephen Curry on one of the league's best teams sounded pretty good too.

Durant's height turned out to be a blessing, and he worked hard to make the most of it. In 2016–2017, Durant and his Golden State teammates formed one of the most talented groups in recent history. Together, they're on track to be NBA champions.

Durant scores another basket for the Warriors.

All-Star Stats

Kevin Durant was just 25 years old when he was voted **NBA MVP** for the 2013–2014 season. That made him one of the youngest MVPs of all time. See where he ranks on the all-time list:

Youngest NBA MVPs

Age	Player	Team	Season
22	Derrick Rose	Chicago Bulls	2010–2011
23	Bob McAdoo	Buffalo Braves	1974–1975
23	Wes Unseld	Baltimore Bullets	1968–1969
23	Wilt Chamberlain	Philadelphia Warriors	1959–1960
24	LeBron James	Cleveland Cavaliers	2008–2009
24	Moses Malone	Houston Rockets	1978–1979
24	Dave Cowens	Boston Celtics	1972–1973
24	Lew Alcindor	Milwaukee Bucks	1970–1971
24	Bill Russell	Boston Celtics	1957–1958
24	Bob Pettit	St. Louis Hawks	1955–1956
25	Kevin Durant	Oklahoma City Thunder	2013–2014
25	Tim Duncan	San Antonio Spurs	2001–2002
25	Allen Iverson	Philadelphia 76ers	2000–2001
25	Michael Jordon	Chicago Bulls	1987–1988
25	Bill Walton	Portland Trail Blazers	1977–1978
25	Oscar Robertson	Cincinnati Royals	1963–1964

Source Notes

9   Tom Friend, "Kevin Durant Humble in the Heartland," *ESPN*, May 14, 2011, http://www.espn.com/espn/otl /columns/story?id=6530509.

13 Sarah Kogod, "Kevin Durant Shows the World Where He Came From," *Washington Post*, July 1, 2013, https://www.washingtonpost.com/news/dc-sports -bog/wp/2013/07/01/kevin-durant-shows-the-world -where-he-came-from.

14 Jack McCallum, "The Kid Enters the Picture," *Sports Illustrated*, November 6, 2007, http://www.si.com /more-sports/2007/11/06/durant1112.

17 Nina Mandell, "Kevin Durant's Insane Offseason Workouts Include Running Uphill through Sand with Russell Westbrook," *USA Today*, November 3, 2014, http://ftw.usatoday.com/2014/11/kevin-durant-russell -westbrook.

19 Kevin Durant Charity Foundation, accessed October 25, 2016, http://kevindurant.com/foundation

Glossary

draft: a yearly event in which teams take turns choosing players

dumbbells: short bars with weights at each end

endorse: support and appear in advertisements for a company or product

free agent: a player free to sign with any team

layup: a one-handed shot near the basket

lunges: leg exercises in which a person steps forward with both knees bent

National Collegiate Athletic Association (NCAA) men's basketball tournament: games held each year to determine a champion for college basketball's top level

prospect: a player who basketball experts think is likely to succeed at a higher level

rebounds: balls that bounce away from the basket after a missed shot

rookie: a first-year player

trainers: fitness experts who teach athletes

Braun, Eric. *Stephen Curry*. Minneapolis: Lerner Publications, 2017.

Fishman, Jon M. *LeBron James*. Minneapolis: Lerner Publications, 2018.

Gitlin, Marty. *Kevin Durant: Basketball Star*. Mankato, MN: North Star Editions, 2017.

Jr. NBA
http://jr.nba.com

Kevin Durant
http://www.nba.com/players/kevin/durant/201142

Kevin Durant Charity Foundation
http://kevindurant.com/foundation

Index

Cleveland Cavaliers, 6

Curry, Stephen, 6, 26

ESPY award, 22

Golden State Warriors, 5–7, 26–27

Hill, 12–14

James, LeBron, 17

Kevin Durant Charity Foundation, 22

MVP, 6, 25

New Orleans Pelicans, 6–7

Nike, 19–20

Oklahoma City Thunder, 6, 11, 25

salary, 18

San Antonio Spurs, 5

Seattle SuperSonics, 11, 25

TV, 22

University of Texas, 10–11

Westbrook, Russell, 17

working out, 17

Photo Acknowledgments

The images in this book are used with the permission of: © iStockphoto.com/63151 (gold and silver stars); JOHN G. MABANGLO/EPA/Newscom, p. 2; Kyle Terada/ USA Today Sports/Newscom, p. 4; © Jonathan Bachman/Getty Images, pp. 7, 21; © Jay Drowns/Sporting News/Getty Images, p. 8; © Toni L. Sandys/The Washington Post/Getty Images, p. 9; © Jim Redman/WireImage/Getty Images, p. 11; © ANDREJ ISAKOVIC/AFP/Getty Images, p. 12; © Shannon Finney/Getty Images, p. 13; © Ethan Miller/Getty Images, pp. 14, 15; AP Photo/Morry Gash, p. 16; AP Photo/Alex Brandon, p. 17; © VCG/Getty Images, p. 18; © Ronald Martinez/Getty Images, p. 19; © Zhong Zhi/Getty Images, p. 20; © Joe Scarnici/Getty Images, p. 22; John Shearer/Invision/ AP Photo, p. 23; AP Photo/Craig Mitchelldyer, p. 24; AP Photo/Sue Ogrocki, p. 25; © Vaughn Ridley/Getty Images, p. 26; AP Photo/Ross D. Franklin, p. 27.

Front cover: JOHN G. MABANGLO/EPA/Newscom; © iStockphoto.com/neyro2008 (motion lines). **31901062936754**